Tundra Animals

Biome B

Lisa Colozza Cocca

Rourke
Educational Media
rourkeeducationalmedia.com

A Division of
Carson
Dellosa
Education

Before Reading: *Building Background Knowledge and Vocabulary*

Building background knowledge can help children process new information and build upon what they already know. Before reading a book, it is important to tap into what children already know about the topic. This will help them develop their vocabulary and increase their reading comprehension.

Questions and Activities to Build Background Knowledge:

1. Look at the front cover of the book and read the title. What do you think this book will be about?
2. What do you already know about this topic?
3. Take a book walk and skim the pages. Look at the table of contents, photographs, captions, and bold words. Did these text features give you any information or predictions about what you will read in this book?

Vocabulary: *Vocabulary Is Key to Reading Comprehension*

Use the following directions to prompt a conversation about each word.

- Read the vocabulary words.
- What comes to mind when you see each word?
- What do you think each word means?

Vocabulary Words:

- burrow
- colonies
- dormant
- hibernate
- lichens
- migrate
- precipitation
- prey
- subsoil
- undercoat

During Reading: *Reading for Meaning and Understanding*

To achieve deep comprehension of a book, children are encouraged to use close reading strategies. During reading, it is important to have children stop and make connections. These connections result in deeper analysis and understanding of a book.

 Close Reading a Text

During reading, have children stop and talk about the following:

- Any confusing parts
- Any unknown words
- Text to text, text to self, text to world connections
- The main idea in each chapter or heading

Encourage children to use context clues to determine the meaning of any unknown words. These strategies will help children learn to analyze the text more thoroughly as they read.

When you are finished reading this book, turn to the next-to-last page for Text-Dependent Questions and an Extension Activity.

Table of Contents

Biomes

A biome is a large region of Earth with living things that have adapted to the conditions of that region.

Tundra biomes are cold, dry regions. Few reptiles or amphibians live in tundra biomes because the biomes are too cold.

☐ = Tundra

NORTH AMERICA

SOUTH AMERICA

Did You Know?

Tundra plants include short bushes, grasses, flowers, mosses, and **lichens**. The growth cycle is short—less than two months.

The Arctic tundra is located around the North Pole. Summers are cold and winters are freezing. There is little **precipitation**.

The top layer of soil in the Arctic tundra goes through a freeze and defrost cycle. Under the topsoil is a layer of permafrost. This is a layer of **subsoil** that has remained frozen for at least two years.

EUROPE

ASIA

ICA

AUSTRALIA

The alpine tundra is located above the tree line on tall, cold mountains. Summers here are cool and winters are cold. There is less precipitation here than in the Arctic tundra.

Out and About

Despite the harsh conditions, many animals remain active year-round. Polar bears live in the Arctic tundra. Their large size, thick white fur, and thick layer of fat lower heat loss. Under the white fur is a layer of black skin that soaks in the sun's heat.

Fur on the soles of the feet gives polar bears a better grip when walking on ice and helps keep their paws warm. Their paws are also webbed for swimming in the nearby ocean.

The polar bear's white fur blends in with the snow and ice. This makes it harder for its **prey** to see it coming. The bear eats mainly seals, but also eats fish and other mammals.

Did You Know?

The polar bear doesn't need to worry about hiding from predators. It is so big that it has no natural predators in the tundra.

Musk oxen also live in the Arctic tundra. Their long, shaggy hair and thick, wooly **undercoat** keep them warm in the winter. In the summer, the undercoat falls out.

Did You Know?

Musk oxen work as a community when threatened. They form a circle around their young and stand with their sharp horns pointing out. They charge at predators with great force if necessary.

Musk oxen are plant eaters. In the summer, they
eat flowers and grasses. In the winter, they dig
through the snow with their hooves to reach roots,
mosses, and lichens.

Arctic foxes live in both Arctic and alpine tundra biomes. Their thick fur is brown in summer and white in winter. Their furry soles keep their paws warm. During a blizzard, they **burrow** into snow for shelter.

Arctic foxes can hear prey moving under snow and know its exact location. The fox then pounces on the snow, breaks through it, and lands on its prey. In the Arctic tundra, the fox will also follow a polar bear and eat its leftovers.

Ibex are sure-footed wild goats. These strong jumpers live in alpine tundra biomes. They have thick brown to gray fur. Males have beards and

In the summertime, they look for plants to eat in the morning and evening. The ibex rest during the warmest part of the day. Food is more difficult to find in winter, so

Under Cover

Some animals in the tundra live mainly underground. The lemming is a small mouse-like animal in the Arctic tundra. Its thick, coarse fur helps to keep it warm. This plant-eater has sharp teeth for eating tough roots.

In the summertime, the lemming travels through a maze of tunnels and passageways through the plants on the ground. In the winter, its claws grow longer so it can dig tunnels through the snow.

Ermines live in the alpine tundra. These nocturnal animals dig dens and tunnels underground. Ermines use their keen senses to hunt. They can smell hares and rodents, hear insects, and see fish at night.

Did You Know?

The ermine must eat every day, so it builds an extra room in its den to store food.

Females hunt mainly underground where they are safer. Males spend much time hunting above ground and are often caught by predators.

Pikas also live in the alpine tundra. These mammals are in the same family as rabbits. They have egg-shaped bodies and thick, brown-gray hair. Their toes are padded for running on rocks.

Did You Know?

Pikas screech "eek" to warn other pikas that a predator is nearby.

Pikas live in groups called **colonies** in underground burrows. In the summer, they go out during the cooler hours of the day to look for plants to eat. They store extra food in piles called *haystacks*. At the end of summer, they move the haystacks into their burrows.

Hibernation

Some members of tundra biomes **hibernate** to survive the coldest times. The Arctic ground squirrel hibernates for seven months at a time. In September, it burrows about three feet (one meter) underground. Every two or three weeks, it shivers and shakes for about 15 hours. The movement does not pull the squirrel out of hibernation. It raises the squirrel's body temperature, so it doesn't freeze to death.

Alpine marmots live underground in a series of tunnels with a large den in the center. They spend each spring and summer eating to prepare for hibernation. In October, their long hibernation begins. They wake about every ten days for a few hours to raise their body temperature.

Did You Know?

Alpine marmot families line their den with hay and seal off the entrance with mud for the winter. Then they cuddle together in the center to hibernate.

Part-Time Members

Many animals can survive in a tundra biome for only part of the year. Arctic bumblebees are hairier than most bumblebees. Their thick fur helps trap body heat. Their large flat wing muscles move very quickly to raise their body temperature.

The queen bee produces many new queen bees, but usually only one survives. The rest of the colony dies when summer ends. The new queen bee moves underground into a mouse hole. It goes **dormant** for nine months before starting a new bee colony.

Did You Know?

The Arctic tundra has only two seasons—summer and winter. Summer lasts only one to two months. The sun is up almost 24 hours a day during that time, but the air remains cold.

Snow geese breed in the Arctic tundra. They dig nests in the defrosted topsoil and lay their eggs. After the chicks hatch, they can swim and eat on their own within 24 hours. The geese fly south to warmer areas at the end of the short summer.

Did You Know?

A snow goose has a black line that stretches from its bill across its face. It makes this white bird look like it is always grinning.

Caribou, or reindeer, can sniff lichen under two feet (61 centimeters) of snow. They dig through snow with their hooves and antlers to reach the food.

During the coldest months, caribou often **migrate** south to the boreal forest to find food. They return to the tundra in spring.

The harsh conditions of the tundra limit the number of living things that can make their homes here. However, even in the Arctic tundra, which has the coldest climate on Earth, some animals have adapted to survive and thrive in this challenging biome.

ACTIVITY: Make a Better Boot

Inventors often look at nature for ideas on how to improve the things we use every day. Think about the different hooves and paws the animals in the tundra have. What adaptations make travel on the frozen ground easier? Use what you have learned to design a better boot that will make it easier for people to walk on ice without slipping or falling.

Supplies

- baking pan
- water
- paper and pencil
- wooden block
- tape
- scissors
- scraps of craft fur and foam, pencil erasers, cork, rubber bands, or other materials

Directions

1. Fill the pan with water and freeze it.
2. Use the pencil and paper to design a boot based on the animal feet described in this book and on the scrap materials you have collected.
3. Imagine that the block is a foot. Cut scrap materials to cover the foot and make a boot.
4. Use tape loops, sticky side out, to attach the materials to the block.
5. Test your boot design by moving it across the pan of ice.

Repeat your experiment with different designs and materials. Which will work best for walking on a frozen surface?

Glossary

burrow (BUR-oh): to dig a tunnel or hole and hide inside

colonies (KAH-luh-neez): groups of animals that live together

dormant (DOR-muhnt): in a state of hibernation in which body functions slow down

hibernate (HYE-bur-nate): to go into a deep sleep in which heart rate and breathing slow down and body temperature drops

lichens (LYE-kuhnz): algae and fungi growing closely together on trees, rocks, and walls

migrate (MYE-grate): to move from one area to another

precipitation (pri-sip-i-TAY-shuhn): water that falls from clouds in the form of rain, snow, sleet, or hail

prey (pray): an animal that is hunted by another animal for food

subsoil (suhb-SOIL): soil under the topsoil

undercoat (UHN-dur-koht): short hair or fur partly covered by longer hair or fur on a mammal

Tundra Animals

Biome Beasts

Lisa Colozza Cocca

Bridges